Pastor Char[...]

T[...]

coming to

Monroe

May God continue

to guide & direct

your Path

In His Love

Carol

Longenberger

To:

_____

From:

_____

© 2011 by Barbour Publishing, Inc.

Compiled by Kathy Shutt.

ISBN 978-1-61626-396-6

Scripture quotations marked KJV are taken from the King James Version of the Bible.

Scripture quotations marked NIV are taken from the HOLY BIBLE, NEW INTERNATIONAL VERSION®. NIV®. Copyright © 1973, 1978, 1984, 2010 by Biblica, Inc. ™ Used by permission. All rights reserved worldwide.

Cover and Interior Design: Thinkpen Design, Inc., www.thinkpendesign.com

Published by Barbour Publishing, Inc., P.O. Box 719, Uhrichsville, Ohio 44683, www.barbourbooks.com

Our mission is to publish and distribute inspirational products offering exceptional value and biblical encouragement to the masses.

 Member of the
Evangelical Christian
Publishers Association

Printed in China.

Joy to the World

Music & Inspiration to Celebrate the Season

BARBOUR

Joy to the world, the Lord is come!
Let earth receive her King;
Let every heart prepare Him room,
And heaven and nature sing,
And heaven and nature sing,
And heaven, and heaven, and nature sing.

Isaac Watts

Celebrate the season. . .
for nature gives to
every time and season
some beauties of its own.

CHARLES DICKENS

Ah, friends, dear friends, as years go on and
heads get gray, how fast the guests do go!
Touch hands, touch hands, with those who stay.
Strong hands to weak, old hands to young,
around the Christmas board, touch hands.
The false forget, the foe forgive, for every guest
will go and the fire burn low and cabin empty
stand. Forget, forgive, for who may say that
Christmas Day may ever come again.
Touch hands!

WILLIAM HENRY HARRISON MURRAY

May you find joy
in the Messiah's birth
and exult in a renewed
spirit throughout the
coming new year.

DEBORAH BOONE

And Mary said, My soul doth magnify the Lord, and my spirit hath rejoiced in God my Saviour.

LUKE 1:46–47 KJV

Time was with most of us, when
Christmas Day, encircling all our
limited world like a magic ring,
left nothing out for us to miss or
seek; bound together all our home
enjoyments, affections, and hopes;
grouped everything and everyone
round the Christmas fire; and made
the little picture shining in our
bright young eyes, complete.

CHARLES DICKENS

May you
find joy—not only
at Christmastime—
but in the everyday
miracles of Life.

K. McIntosh

"She will give birth to a son, and you are to give him the name Jesus, because he will save his people from their sins."

MATTHEW 1:21 NIV

Listen to the angel's song, all you who have a troubled heart. "I bring you good tidings of great joy!" Never let the thought cross your mind that Christ is angry with you! He did not come to condemn you. If you want to define Christ rightly, then pay heed to how the angel defines Him: namely, "A great joy!"

MARTIN LUTHER

This is Christmas: not the tinsel,
not the giving and receiving,
not even the carols, but the humble
heart that receives anew the
wondrous gift, the Christ.

FRANK MCKIBBEN

Until one feels the spirit of
Christmas, there is no Christmas.
All else is outward display—
so much tinsel and decorations.
For it isn't the holly, it isn't the snow.
It isn't the tree, nor the firelight's glow.
It's the warmth that comes
to the hearts of men
When the Christmas spirit
returns again.

UNKNOWN

After Jesus was born in Bethlehem in Judea, during the time of King Herod, Magi from the east came to Jerusalem and asked, "Where is the one who has been born king of the Jews? We saw his star when it rose and have come to worship him."

MATTHEW 2:1–2 NIV

Smiles. Small kindnesses
extended. A neighbor bringing
a plate of cookies.
A piano playing Christmas
carols in a department store.
Cups of wassail offered
in places of business. . .

Clerks and customers wishing
each other Merry Christmas
and Happy Holidays!
Wouldn't it be wonderful if
this thoughtfulness lasted
throughout the year?
Maybe it could start with me.

DEBORAH BOONE

What I'd like to
have for Christmas
I can tell you in a minute
The family all around me
And the home with
Laughter in it.

EDGAR A. GUEST

From home to home, and heart to heart, from one place to another. The warmth and joy of Christmas brings us closer to each other.

EMILY MATTHEWS

For unto us a child is born, unto us a son is given: and the government shall be upon his shoulder: and his name shall be called Wonderful, Counsellor, The mighty God, The everlasting Father, The Prince of Peace.

ISAIAH 9:6 KJV

I heard the bells on Christmas Day,
their old familiar carols play,
And wild and sweet the words repeat
of peace on earth, goodwill to men!

HENRY WADSWORTH LONGFELLOW

When they saw the star,
they were overjoyed. . . .
They saw the child with his
mother Mary, and they bowed
down and worshiped him.
Then they opened their treasures
and presented him with gifts.

Matthew 2:10–11 niv

As with gladness, men of old
Did the guiding star behold
As with joy they hailed its light
Leading onward, beaming bright
So, most glorious Lord, may we
Evermore be led to Thee.

WILLIAM C. DIX

Somehow, not only at Christmas,
but all the long year through,
The joy that you give to others is the
joy that comes back to you.

JOHN GREENLEAF WHITTIER

What is Christmas?
It is a fervent wish that
every cup may overflow
with blessings rich and
eternal, and that every
path may lead to peace.

AGNES M. PHARO

*And, lo, the angel of the Lord
came upon them, and the glory of
the Lord shone round about them:
and they were sore afraid. And the
angel said unto them, Fear not:
for, behold, I bring you good
tidings of great joy, which
shall be to all people.*

LUKE 2:9–10 KJV

Let us remember that the Christmas heart is a giving heart, a wide open heart that thinks of others first. The birth of the baby Jesus stands as the most significant event in all history, because it has meant the pouring into a sick world of the healing medicine of love which has transformed all manner of hearts for almost two thousand years. . . .

Underneath all the bulging bundles is this beating Christmas heart.

GEORGE MATTHEW ADAMS

"Glory to God in the highest heaven, and on earth peace to those on whom his favor rests."

Luke 2:14 niv

Hold God's love in your heart...
And spread His love to others
This holiday season—and always.

K. McIntosh

Best of all, Christmas means a spirit
of love, a time when the love of
God and the love of our fellow men
should prevail over all hatred and
bitterness, a time when our thoughts
and deeds and the spirit of our lives
manifest the presence of God.

George F. McDougall

Love came down at Christmas,
Love all lovely, love divine;
Love was born at Christmas;
Star and angels gave the sign.

CHRISTINA ROSSETTI

More than two thousand years ago,
the angels brought their glad tidings
to a bunch of shepherds who were
huddled with their sheep on a cold hillside.
The Son of God is born! the angels sang
on that long-ago dark night. . . .

On the darkest, coldest nights this world offers, Jesus can be birthed anew in our own hearts—and in Him we will find an entirely new way to love. No longer will we put ourselves at the center of the world; no longer will we push and shove to get what we want. Instead, we will follow a new path—the path of love.

ELLYN SANNA

Silent night, holy night,
all is calm, all is bright,
round yon virgin mother and child.
Holy infant so tender and mild,
sleep in heavenly peace,
sleep in heavenly peace.
Silent night, holy night,
all is calm, all is bright,
round yon virgin mother and child.
Holy infant so tender and mild,
sleep in heavenly peace,
sleep in heavenly peace.

JOSEF MOHR

And a little child will lead them.

ISAIAH 11:6 NIV

O come all ye faithful,
joyful and triumphant,
O come ye, O come ye,
to Bethlehem;
Come and behold Him,
born the King of angels.
O come, let us adore Him,
Christ the Lord.

JOHN FRANCIS WADE

Our lives are destined to become
like the life of Jesus. The whole purpose
of Jesus' ministry is to bring us to the
house of the Father. Not only did Jesus
come to free us from the bonds of sin
and death, He also came to lead us
into the intimacy of His divine life.

HENRI NOUWEN

Blessed is the
season which
engages the whole
world in a
conspiracy of love.

HAMILTON WRIGHT MABI

An angel of the Lord appeared to him in a dream and said, "Joseph son of David, do not be afraid to take Mary home as your wife, because what is conceived in her is from the Holy Spirit. She will give birth to a son, and you are to give him the name Jesus, because he will save his people from their sins."

. . .All this took place to fulfill what the Lord had said through the prophet: "The virgin will conceive and give birth to a son, and they will call him Immanuel" (which means "God with us").

MATTHEW 1:20–23 NIV

Christmas evokes so many emotions. . .fond memories of Christmases past, pleasure in the present, hope for the future.

DEBORAH BOONE

Take time this Christmastide
to go a little way apart,
And with the help of God prepare
the house that is in your heart.

ANONYMOUS

May no gift be too small
to give, nor too simple to receive,
which is wrapped in thoughtfulness,
and tied with love.

L. O. BAIRD

Christmas—that magic blanket that wraps itself about us, that something so intangible that it is like a fragrance. It may weave a spell of nostalgia. Christmas may be a day of feasting, or a day of prayer, but always it will be a day of remembrance—a day in which we think of everything we have ever loved.

AUGUSTA E. RUNDEL

Dear Lord,
Help me to keep my eyes
fixed on You throughout
the Christmas season.
When the commercialism of
the holiday threatens to snuff
out the real meaning of Christmas
in my heart, remind me of the
gift of hope You sent on that
silent night so long ago. Amen.

K. McIntosh

O come, let us worship
and bow down: Let us kneel
before the L<small>ORD</small> our maker.

P<small>SALM</small> 95:6 <small>KJV</small>

O little town of Bethlehem,
how still we see thee lie!
Above thy deep and dreamless
sleep the silent stars go by.
Yet in thy dark streets shineth
the everlasting light;
the hopes and fears of all the
years are met in thee tonight.

PHILLIPS BROOKS

I am never alone at all, I thought.
I was never alone at all. And that,
of course, is the message of
Christmas. We are never alone.
Not when the night is darkest,
the wind coldest, the world
seemingly most indifferent.
For this is still the time God chooses.

TAYLOR CALDWELL

Oh, thank You, Jesus, for being born for us,
and living for us, and dying for us, and rising for
us, and sending us the Holy Spirit.
Thank You, with thanks beyond words, but must
be expressed in the lovingness of our lives.

MADELEINE L'ENGLE

And ransom captive Israel,
That mourns in lonely exile here
Until the Son of God appear.
Rejoice! Rejoice!
Emmanuel shall come to thee,
O Israel.

Latin Hymn

We have peace with God through our Lord Jesus Christ.

ROMANS 5:1 NIV

Angels we have heard on high
sweetly singing o'er the plains,
and the mountains in reply echoing
their joyous strains.
Gloria, in Excelsis Deo!
Gloria, in Excelsis Deo!

Shepherds, why this jubilee?
Why your joyous strains prolong?
What the gladsome tidings be which
inspire your heavenly song?
Gloria, in Excelsis Deo!
Gloria, in Excelsis Deo! . . .

Come to Bethlehem and see Christ
whose birth the angels sing;
Come adore on bended knee, Christ
the Lord, the newborn King.

Advent is the perfect time to clear and prepare the way. Advent is a winter training camp for those who desire peace. By reflection and prayer, by reading and meditation, we can make our hearts a place where a blessing of peace would desire to abide and where the birth of the Prince of Peace might take place.

EDWARD HAYS

Amid all the festivities of
the season, don't forget to make
room for Him in your heart. The Lord
wants to spend time with you—to
know you intimately. Make room for
Him, and He will bless you far beyond
anything you can imagine!

DEBORAH BOONE

Are you willing to believe that
love is the strongest thing in the
world—stronger than hate, stronger
than evil, stronger than death—
and that the blessed life which
began in Bethlehem nineteen
hundred years ago is the image and
brightness of the eternal love?
Then you can keep Christmas.

HENRY VAN DYKE

The joy of brightening other
lives, bearing each other's burdens,
easing other's loads and supplanting
empty hearts and lives with
generous gifts becomes for us
the magic of Christmas.

W. C. JONES

Celebrate the happiness that friends are always giving, make every day a holiday, and celebrate just living!

AMANDA BRADLEY

The day and the spirit of Christmas
rearrange the world parade. As the
world arranges it, usually there come
first in importance—leading the
parade with a big blare of a band—
the big shots. . . . Then at the tail end,
as of little importance, trudge
the weary, the poor, the lame,
the halt, and the blind. . . .

But in the Christmas spirit,
the procession is turned around.
Those at the tail end are put first
in the arrangement of the
Child of Christmas.

HALFORD E. LUCCOCK

Increasingly I rejoiced in the
gospel—the amazing good news—
that the Creator of what to us human
beings is this bewildering and
unimaginably vast universe,
so loved the world that He gave His
only Son, that whosoever believes
in Him should not perish,
but have everlasting life. . . .

Everlasting life, I came to see,
is not just continued existence but
a growing knowledge—not merely
intellectual but wondering through
trust, love, and fellowship—of Him
who alone is truly God, and Jesus
Christ whom He has sent.

Kenneth Scott Latourette

When He sent us His Son, God crossed the distance that once separated human beings from Him. Our King came to live with us. No wonder Christmas is a day of joy!

ELLYN SANNA

Let the heavens rejoice
and the earth be glad before
the Lord, for He comes.

FROM THE
Offertory of the Christmas Mass,
BASED ON PSALM 96:11, 13 NIV

Exactly as though it were morning
and not the night, the shepherds
went out into the city and began
immediately to tell everyone what
the angel had said about this child.
They left a trail of startled people
behind them, as on they went, both
glorifying and praising God.

WALTER WANGERIN JR.

Once in royal David's city
Stood a lovely cattle shed,
Where a mother laid her baby
In a manger for His bed:
Mary was that mother mild,
Jesus Christ her little child.

CECIL FRANCES ALEXANDER

And she brought forth her firstborn son, and wrapped him in swaddling clothes, and laid him in a manger.

LUKE 2:7 KJV

Away in a manger,
No crib for a bed,
The little Lord Jesus
Laid down His sweet head.
The stars in the sky
Looked down where He lay,
The little Lord Jesus,
Asleep on the hay. . . .

Be near me, Lord Jesus,
I ask Thee to stay
Close by me forever,
And love me I pray;
Bless all the dear children
In Thy tender care,
And fit us for heaven
To live with Thee there.

ANONYMOUS

Like the shepherds who heard
the angels' wonderful tidings, we, too,
can forget the night we see around
us. We know the day has dawned.
If you commit yourself to this belief,
those around you may be as startled
and disbelieving as those who
heard the shepherds' news.
But why walk in the darkness
anymore when the Christmas
star shines bright as day?

ELLYN SANNA

And the Word was made flesh,
and dwelt among us,
(and we beheld his glory).

JOHN 1:14 KJV

The child who was born so long
ago came because He loves you.
He wants to give Himself to you.
He was born *for you.*

ELLYN SANNA

Hark! The herald angels sing
"Glory to the newborn King;
Peace on earth, and mercy mild,
God and sinners reconciled!"
Joyful, all ye nations rise,
Join the triumph of the skies;
With th' angelic host proclaim
Christ is born in Bethlehem.

CHARLES WESLEY

Sometimes the glad tidings
of Christmas seem simply too
good to be true. But. . .as you keep
quiet and listen, you will know deep
down in your heart that you are
loved. As the air is around about you,
so is His love around you. Trust
that love. . . . It will never fail.

AMY CARMICHAEL

We also have the prophetic message as something completely reliable, and you will do well to pay attention to it, as to a light shining in a dark place, until the day dawns and the morning star rises in your hearts.

2 PETER 1:19 NIV

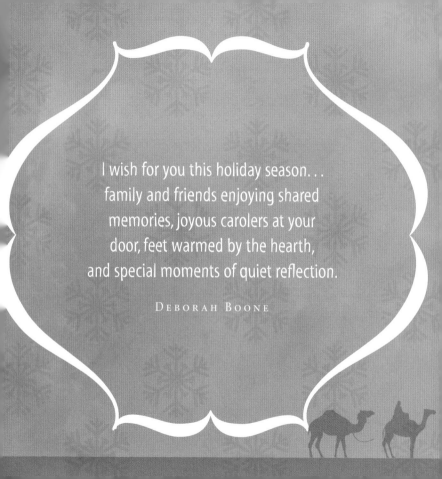

I wish for you this holiday season. . .
family and friends enjoying shared
memories, joyous carolers at your
door, feet warmed by the hearth,
and special moments of quiet reflection.

DEBORAH BOONE

Celebration is the recognition
that something is there and needs
to be made visible so that
we can say yes to it.

HENRI M. NOUWEN

I will honor Christmas in my heart and try to keep it all the year.

EBENEZER SCROOGE
A Christmas Carol BY CHARLES DICKENS

Lord Jesus, please forgive me for being grumpy as I trudge through the never-ending tasks set before me this holiday season. My to-do list seems to keep growing with shopping, church services, and family gatherings—and I'm running short on time! Restore the joy of Christmas to my heart. . .and help me to relax each day and make time for You, my one true Source of Joy.

K. McIntosh

For he himself is our peace.

Ephesians 2:14 niv

How can we claim to have…
"good news," unless people can
see in us that Jesus Christ is
breaking down the barriers
and bringing us together?

ALBERT BRAITHWAITE

Christmas...is not an eternal event
at all, but a piece of one's home that
one carries in one's heart.

FREYA STARK

At Christmas, play
and make good cheer
For Christmas comes
but once a year.

THOMAS TUSSER

*Suddenly a great company of
the heavenly host appeared with
the angel, praising God and saying,
"Glory to God in the highest
heaven, and on earth peace to those
on whom his favor rests."*

. . .When the angels had left
them and gone into heaven,
the shepherds said to one another,
"Let's go to Bethlehem and see this
thing that has happened,
which the Lord has told us about."

LUKE 2:13–15 NIV

May you have
the gladness of Christmas,
which is hope;
The spirit of Christmas,
which is peace;
The heart of Christmas,
which is Love.

AVA V. HENDRICKS